Transcendence

A Collection of Poems and Short Stories

Barbara Voegeli

Copyright © 2024 Barbara Voegeli

Published by CaryPress International Books

www.CaryPress.com

All rights reserved. No part of this publication may be reproduced, distributed, or transmitted in any form or by any means, including photocopying, recording, or other electronic or mechanical methods, without the prior written permission of the publisher, except in the case of brief quotations embodied in critical reviews and certain other non-commercial uses permitted by copyright law.

DEDICATION

This book is dedicated to Barbara's grandchildren, Bobby, Becky, and Daniel

TABLE OF CONTENTS

The Miracle	1
ANIMALS FROM A TO Z	3
Backyard Squirrels	14
Bird Brain	16
Boo-Boo	22
Jump, Froggy, Jump!	31
Poem Collection:	
Heartstrings Haiku	33
Crow	33
April	34
Tanka	35
December	35
Spring Song	35
Snow Drops	36
Sunbeam	36
Sentinel Oak	37
Japan	37
Japanese Garden	38
Cardinal in Winter	38
Bumblebee Morning	38
Bumblebee Evening	39
Autumn	39
Farewell to Summer	39
Autumn Tableau	40
Marco Evening	40
Butler Park Pond	40
Spring Song	41
Guardian Wolf	41
April	41
Ancient Oak	42

Hibiscus	43
Arkansas Dawn	43
Egret	43
Summer Shower	44
Playful Breeze	44
Summer's Face	44
Monday at the Botanic Garden	45
Seagull Respite	45
Winter Frost	45
Premonition	46
Deer Path	46
Bird Gleaners	46
Winter Overture	47
Goddess of the Night	47
Fireflies	47
September Song	48
Sunset at Lake Michigan	48
Ravine Patterns	49
Lake Michigan	49
Jack in the Pulpit	50
Outer Banks	50
Winter Photo	51
Sansho En	51
Backyard Portrait	52
Swans	52
Rosewood Beach	53
Weeping Willow	53
Sheridan Road	54
Broken Oak	54
Lake Michigan Afternoon	54
God's Cathedral	55
Vigil	55

Lumberjacks Camp	56
Project Linus	56
October Evening	57
Summer Morning	57
Storm	57
Mystic Trees	58
Abrupt Winter	60
Night	60
Broken Horse	61
Autumn Tapestry	61
Illinois Tanka	62
Song of the Shore	63
Love	64
Broken Horse	65
Poem Collection:	
Snowdrops	66
Fireflies	66
December	66
Sculpture	67
Spring Fanfare	67
Lake Michigan Sunset	68
Autumn Tableau	68
Winter Cathedral	69
Haiku: Traditional	69
Rainbow in My Web	70
I Know You	71
Agape	72
Transcendence	74
Karma	75
Ballad of the Bugs	76

She Fell in the Vat of Molasses	78
Portrait of March	80
The Mermaid	81
Dear Beacky, Bobby, and Daniel	82
The Rose	84
Song of the Shore	86
Journey's End	87
Star Path	88
Round is the Sun	89
You are my Sunshine	91
The Fairy Queen	93
Winter's Tale	96
Robins in the Maple Tree	97
A Spider Danced	98
Sir Lancelot's Debut	100
Scarlet	101
Libertyville Civic Center	102
Star of the Week	103
Theater on the Lake	108
Tea, Anyone?	110
The Little Christmas Tree in the Forest	111
Toogie and Bob	117
We're All Winners	121
About the Author	125
Awards	127

The Miracle

Angels announced a miracle one starry night.

Bethlehem was to be the birthplace of the savior.

Calm reigned throughout Palestine on this holy night.

Dazzling stars blinked against a dark velvet sky.

Each star paled in the brilliant light of a new star.

From the east, three kings on camels followed the star.

Gold, frankincense and myrrh they brought.

Home for the baby on his first night was a rude stable.

In the stable was a manger filled with hay.

Jesus, the baby king, claimed it for his bed.

Kneeling before the manger, the kings presented their gifts.

Lambs entered the stable to look at the holy child.

Mary and Joseph welcomed them with loving smiles.

Nearby the shepherds knelt and watched in awe.

Overhead the star gave promise of peace on earth.

Praising God, the shepherds returned to their flocks.

Quiet lay over the little town of Bethlehem.

Reverently, the kings left for home.

Softly, the night wind whispered of good will toward men.

Town of Bethlehem, God chose you for the birthplace of His son.

Under heaven you are the place forever blessed by angels and men.

Virgin birth is a mystery we still ponder after two thousand years.

Wondrous Holy Spirit, your love is made manifest in the Son.

X is the Greek symbol for Christos, and so Christmas is also Xmas.

Yuletide is another name for the season of Christmas.

Zion is the heaven promised to those who live the miracle.

ANIMALS FROM A TO Z

        A is for Alligator

A is for alligator. Look at him grin.

    No way would I tickle *him* under the chin!

He lies there all sleepy eyed, as nice as can be,

    But fall in the swamp and he'll have you for tea!

        B is for Beaver

Beaver is working ever so hard, just as busy as "you know who."

    He never takes a coffee break. That's a fine how do you do!

Gnawing off branches and gluing with mud, he makes a fine hodge-podge,

    Then floats it on the water to create a cozy lodge.

C is for Camel

The camel's back has a very large bump

    And a very strange name   we call it a hump.

He sometimes has two humps but never has three.

    A humpy, bumpy camel is a funny sight to see.

D is for Dog

The dog, we have heard, is our very best friend.

    He's loyal and playful, beginning to end.

Ready to walk with you, nighttime or day.

    Good times or bad he'll be true, come what may.

E is for Elephant

The elephant's trunk is a very long nose
    And up and down is the way it goes.
        It sniffs and it sneezes,
            It sprays if it pleases,
                That wonderful, wiggly nose.

F is for Frog

Frog sits still on the green lily pad.
    He's hoping for lunch on the fly.
        One flick of frog's tongue
            And mosquito's undone.
                For frog it's just pie in the sky.

G is for Giraffe

Giraffe has a very long neck, if you please,
      To reach for the yummiest leaves on the trees.
When he is thirsty he bends way, way down
      To drink from the river or puddles on the ground.

H is for Hippopotamus

When swimming underwater hippopotamus needs no guide.
      He's often called the water horse and keeps eyes open wide.
Olympic medal swimmer? No, in fact, he's rather slow.
      But watch out when he's running. Then it's ready, set, go!

I is for Impala

Impala, the champion antelope, his grace beyond compare.
      While racing with the wind he jumps and seems to float on air.
Running and leaping for the sky, he dances a fine ballet.
      No pirouettes or fancy turns, just impala grand jete.

J is for Jackrabbit

Jackrabbit is a bunny, and he has such long ears

    I can only imagine the things that he hears.

He can run like the wind, and just look at him bound!

    He can leap twenty feet before touching the ground.

K is for Kangaroo

Hooray for Mama Kangaroo! She has a built in couch.

    She has a special pocket in her tummy, called a pouch.

There she cradles Baby, soft and cozy, deep inside,

    Where Baby naps and has a snack, or goes along for the ride.

L is for Lion

The lion, all the experts say, is a jungle king of sorts.
    He wears no crown upon his head, but a bushy mane he sports.
He lies around the livelong day just being a kingly beast,
    While the lioness does his share, and hers, to prepare a tasty feast.

M is for Manatee

The manatee is a swimmer, the mermaid in tales of old.
    She makes her home in places where the water is never cold.
A peaceful life is what she likes, she doesn't like a dare.
    Attention, all you motor boats: Go slowly, please. Take care!

N is for Narwhal

A long and twisted ivory tusk adorns the narwhal's head.
    Though no one knows the reason why, it fills the fish with dread.
It's a very clever spear, I think, for keeping foes at bay.
    Perhaps it's just a handy bat for water baseball play.

O is for Opossum

Opossum is an animal that likes to play the clown.
    He curls his tail around a branch and hangs there, upside down.
When danger's near he lies so still, pretending that he's dead.
    Playing possum keeps him safe, no need for fear or dread.

P is for Panda

The black and white panda that we visit at the zoo
    Dearly loves to snack on tender pieces of bamboo.
Though raccoon is his cousin, panda looks just like a bear.
    Someday if you're in China you may even see him there.

Q is for Quetzal

The quetzal is a lovely bird with wings of green and blue.
    The feathers on his underside are shades of scarlet hue.
His long, proud tail floats up and down whenever he takes flight,
    And curls around him snugly as he guards the nest at night.

R is for Raccoon

Raccoon's face has a mask of black. He's the bandit of the wood.
    He likes to tumble garbage cans as he looks for something good.
No matter where he finds his meals, his mother's words repeat:
    "Remember, dear, to wash your food and paws before you eat."

S is for Sloth

While eating flowers, fruit or leaves sloth never sees the ground.
    He's happy looking at the sky and hanging upside down.
Moving very slowly using two toes, sometimes three,
    He climbs among the branches of a tall rainforest tree.

T is for Turtle

The turtle's shell is a backpack of sorts
    That often comes in handy.
        If he needs to hide, turtle ducks inside.
            Now the backpack's a house, fine and dandy.

U is for Unicorn

Who's the most beautiful horse ever born?

    The fairy tale steed that we call unicorn.

Uni means one. Has he one ear of corn?

    O, no! He's a magical horse with one horn.

V is for Vervet

There's a monkey known as vervet with black feet, hands and face.

    He spy-hops across the African grass at a truly lively pace.

Are enemies near? He can signal or call to sound a speedy alarm.

    Friends and family take to the trees before they come to harm.

W is for Whale

Through the blow hole in his head the whale breathes in and out.

      When whale blows out a great big breath, he makes a waterspout.

In days of old whale lived on land but now lives in the sea,

      And swims with tail and flippers in a life both wild and free.

X is for eXotic

The griffin is quite exotic, a creature that no eyes have seen.

      Neither an eagle nor a lion, but somewhere in between.

Half an eagle and half a lion – how astonishing that would be!

      Perhaps griffin flies, perhaps he roars. It remains a great mystery.

Y is for Yak

The yak is an ox, and he lives in Tibet.

The strangest animal that I've ever met!

His big, hairy body could be a big mop

Except for two horns that stick out at the top!

Z is for Zebra

The zebra wears p.j.'s with stripes black and white.

He wears them all day, and he wears them all night.

"It makes my life so simple," the clever zebra said.

"I never change my clothes, you see, before I go to bed."

Backyard Squirrels

My backyard squirrels are so frisky and busy
        Their antics of Autumn are making me dizzy!

They scamper up trees and then quickly run down
        To gather the acorns that fall to ground.

With sharp little claws they dig right through the grass
        Then drop in their treasures and cover them fast.

When Winter comes calling and frosty winds blow,
        Acorn treasure lies buried beneath the cold snow.

In cozy leaf nests, high on branches of oaks,
        Squirrels sip acorn tea as they tell squirrel jokes.

There's time now for tall tales, at least one or two,

And a tasty hot dinner of boiled acorn stew.

When Springtime returns there's a knock at my door.

Squirrel beggars are here for their peanuts, once more!

October 4, 2003

BIRDBRAIN

Donnie smiled as he put the new birdhouse on the desk in his room. Woodshop was one of his favorite classes in seventh grade. Making the birdhouse had been fun, but he had plans beyond nailing it to a tree in the back yard.

Donnie's brother, Andy, marched into the room uninvited and picked up the birdhouse. Andy was a high school freshman and star pitcher for the park district baseball team. Frowning, he asked, "What's this?"

"The wrens are due back," Donnie said. "If I'm lucky, a couple will move into the birdhouse. I'll keep an eye on them and include the information in my report for science class. By using my woodshop project I can kill two birds with one stone, no pun intended."

Andy snickered and shook his head. "You're a real comedian," he said, "but that doesn't mean you have to be a birdbrain, too. Put up your birdhouse if you have to, but find a different science topic. Something that guys can relate to."

Donnie felt a knot in the pit of his stomach. "Who says guy can't relate to birds?" he asked. "I guess somebody forgot to tell Audubon."

Andy shrugged off Donnie's comment. "You could research baseball stats for your paper, maybe write about the speed of a fast ball or something. I could show you some of my pitches, and you could take some practice hits at the same time. You know. Act like a regular guy."

Donnie took the birdhouse from Andy and pushed him toward the door. "Out!" he ordered.

The next morning Donnie nailed the birdhouse to the maple tree in the back yard. Since it was Saturday, he sat in the family room and watched for early arrivals. Half an hour went by with no sign of migrating birds. Donnie picked up the remote and clicked on the TV.

Andy walked into the family room a few minutes later. "What's that squirrel doing on the birdhouse?" he asked.

"Holy cow!" Donnie yelled. Banging the back door, he flew out of the house and ran across the yard. By the time he reached the birdhouse, the damage had been done. The squirrel's sharp teeth had enlarged the hole, and the weakened perch broke off when Donnie touched it. "It's ruined," he muttered when Andy joined him.

When's your report due?" Andy asked.

"Monday," Donnie said. "I don't know what to do."

"Mr. Breen will cut you some slack," Andy said. "Remember that paper I did when I was in his class? You know, the one about the dimensions of a baseball diamond? He gave me a couple of extra days to work on it, and he promised not to deduct points because it was late." Andy grimaced. "Not that it helped much. I got a C-. Like I said, you could write about something else."

Donnie glared at Andy. "No, thanks. I'm not giving up on my project yet." He went inside and pulled the *Encyclopedia of Birds* from the bookshelf in his room. After scanning several pages, the bluebird caught his eye. Leaving the open book on his bed, Donnie ran to the computer in the family room and clicked on the internet. When he found what he was looking for, he nodded. It just might work. He turned off the computer and headed outside to remove the birdhouse from the maple.

An hour later Andy found him at the workbench in the garage. "What are you doing in here when you could be outside having fun?" he asked.

"Adapting the house for bluebirds," Donnie said. "I made the hole 1 ¼" in diameter, which was the right size for wrens. After the squirrel chewed around the hole, it was 1 ½". That's just right for bluebirds. I'm using sandpaper to smooth the wood around the hole, and I made a new top with a hinge. That way I can open it to see the nest."

"What, no perch?" Andy asked.

"Bluebirds don't need one," Donnie said, "so I sawed off what was left of the perch. When I'm finished, I'll take the birdhouse to the golf course." He felt good about his plan until Andy spoke.

"But not to play golf, right?"

"Yeah," Donnie said, "but wait 'til you hear - - -"

Andy shook his head. "The guys will laugh you off the course when they see you with that birdhouse. I'm meeting some of the team at the park for batting practice. I thought maybe you'd want to go along, but there's no hope for you." Swinging the bat over his shoulder, Andy opened the garage door. "See you later, birdbrain."

As he rode his bike to the golf course, Donnie's anger at Andy's words changed to worry. Maybe Mr. Breen would give him a bad grade on his report, but that was problem number two. First he had to convince the golf pro that his idea was a good one. He would explain how bluebirds like to nest near open fields. Then he would ask for permission to put the birdhouse on a pole or fence post somewhere on the course. Maybe everyone would think he was a real dork, but he'd rather be a birdbrain than a quitter!

Nothing more was said about the birdhouse until Tuesday afternoon. Donnie walked into Andy's room and waved his report in Andy's face. "So I'm a birdbrain, huh?" he said.

Andy grabbed the report. "What's this?" he asked.

"My science report," Donnie said with a grin. "Notice the grade Mr. Breen gave me," he said, "*and* his comment."

Andy whistled. "No kidding! You got an A!" He scanned the comments Mr. Breen had written. "What's this Transcontinental Bluebird Trail?"

"It's a network of bluebird trails across Canada and the United States," Donnie told him. "Members visit the birdhouses at least twice a week from the time the bluebirds mate until the fledglings are on their own. When the parent birds leave to find food, the member assigned to the birdhouse opens the top and reports the number of eggs in the nest. After the eggs hatch, he counts the baby birds and follows their progress. Each week he reports what he sees, and the information is shared on the internet. When I told Mr. Breen that my birdhouse is at the golf course, he agreed to sponsor me as a member of TBT. I promised to report what I see to the class."

Andy hooked his arm around Donnie's neck. "Little brother," he said, "I am *impressed*. As a matter of fact, I have a proposal to make."

Donnie squirmed out of Andy's grasp. "Oh, yeah?" he said.

"Remember that different gifts stuff the minister talked about on Sunday?" Andy asked. "I've been thinking about it."

Donnie picked up the Bible from Andy's desk. "I read the passage again when we got back from church," he said. Flipping through the pages of the New Testament, Donnie stopped at Romans chapter 12. "Here it is in verse 5: 'So we, being many, are one body in Christ, and every one members one of another. Having then gifts differing according to the grace that is given to us.' That's you and me, all right. Different as night and day."

Andy laughed. "I admit I sometimes think you're a little *too* different, but I can't argue with that A on your report. Here's the thing. I'll go to the golf course with you once a week and play bird watcher if you'll agree to play a round of golf while we're there. Loser takes out the garbage for a week. Deal?"

Donnie grinned and shook Andy's hand. "Deal," he said.

BOO-BOO

Scamper the little gray squirrel loved to tease the birds. One morning in November she saw a chance for fun as Owl dozed in the hollow of the pine tree. Climbing stealthily up the tree, Scamper scratched near the hollow with her sharp claws. "Boo! Boo!" she yelled.

Owl opened his eyes wide. "Who? Who?" he screeched.

Scamper giggled. "Not 'who who'," she said. "Boo! Boo! It's only me, silly old Owl!"

Owl glared at her. "Boo, boo, *indeed*," he huffed. "You've disturbed my sleep. *You* are a boo-boo if ever I saw one!"

Scamper stopped giggling. Owl had just told her that she was a foolish mistake! She frowned and ran down the tree. When she reached the ground, Scamper stopped to watch as Chickadee pecked a sunflower seed that had escaped the feeder. A sunflower seed was Scamper's favorite treat, so she jumped on Chickadee's tail. Chickadee was so startled that he dropped the seed. Flapping his wings, he flew to a branch near Owl.

"You frightened me!" Chickadee scolded. Scamper laughed.

"The young ones these days," Owl sighed. "They have no respect for their elders."

"Dee-dee-dee," agreed Chickadee with a nod of his black-capped head. "No wonder Owl called you Boo-Boo," he told Scamper. Ignoring the birds, Scamper put the sunflower seed in her cheek and ran away.

The next morning Scamper returned to the pine tree. Someone had nailed a new wooden bird feeder to the tree. Three holes in the feeder were stuffed with a mixture of peanut butter and sunflower seeds. Chickadee and Wren sat on the perches and pecked at the delicious treat. Scamper crept quietly along the branch above them. Holding onto the branch with her hind feet, Scamper reached down and grabbed an empty perch with her front paws.

The startled birds flew away as the feeder swung wildly back and forth.

"Whee!" shouted Scamper. "This is fun!"

Scamper enjoyed the ride until the feeder stopped swinging. She nibbled on the peanut butter and seeds until the holes were empty. Then she chewed the wood around the holes to get every last bit of peanut butter. Finally, her busy teeth gnawed the perches until they broke and fell to the ground.

"Boo-Boo!" shrieked Chickadee. "You ate up all the food, and you've ruined the feeder, too!"

Scamper looked at the broken feeder then hung her head. "You're right," she said. "I'm sorry."

"Words of sorrow won't feed me," said Wren. "Tomorrow I'll fly south for the winter. Boo-Boo, you're so greedy I've decided not to come back here in the spring. Good luck to you, Chickadee." Wren spread her wings and flew without looking back.

The days grew cold as snow fell and covered the ground. All through the long winter Scamper watched the birds hunt for food. There was never enough, and Chickadee was often hungry. Scamper thought about the secret supply of sunflower seeds she had taken from the birds. She also thought about the acorns she had buried in the fall. There were more than enough acorns to last until spring. It would be hard to give up the sunflower seeds, but Scamper knew what she had to do.

Scamper stuffed her cheeks with seeds and ran to the pine tree. Owl was asleep in his cozy hollow in the tree. Scamper dropped the seeds on the ground beneath the pine tree then hid and waited for Chickadee to find them. Early each winter morning she left a few of her favorite seeds under the pine. Owl was always asleep, and Scamper thought that no one saw what she was doing. By the end of February the seeds were all gone.

On the first warm day of spring Bluebird arrived from the south looking for a new home. Scamper watched him fly to the perch on Wren's birdhouse. He tried to enter the house, but the hole was too small. Bluebird shook his head. "I'll have to go somewhere else," he said.

Scamper remembered how her sharp teeth had ruined the bird feeder. Maybe she could use her teeth again. The birdhouse was made of wood, wasn't it?

Scamper jumped onto a nearby branch. "Wait!" she cried. "Since Wren isn't coming back, she won't be using the house. Maybe I can help."

Bluebird watched Scamper climb to the birdhouse and chew the wood around the hole. Scamper's busy teeth splintered the wood, and the hole became larger. When Scamper had finished, she said, "Now try it."

Bluebird entered the house easily then hopped back outside. "This is the perfect place to raise a family," he said. "Thank you for helping me. What is your name?"

"Scamper," said the little squirrel.

"I'm happy to have you for a neighbor, Scamper," said Bluebird. "I'll be back soon with dried grasses and string to build a nest."

As Bluebird flew away, Chickadee and Owl joined Scamper. "We saw what you did, Scamper," said Chickadee. "I'm happy to call you my neighbor, too."

"Yes, indeed," agreed Owl. "It was you who left the sunflower seeds for Chickadee under the pine tree, wasn't it? That was a great act of kindness, and you never said a word."

Scamper smiled. The birds would never call her Boo-Boo again.

JUMP, FROGGY, JUMP!

Jump, Froggy, jump!

    Into the pond, kerplunk!

The dragonfly

    goes darting by.

        Jump, Froggy, jump!

Hop, Froggy, hop!

    Careful, you'll belly flop!

The spider spins

    The day begins.

        Hop, Froggy, hop!

HEARTSTRINGS HAIKU

Crow

Etched against white snow

Arise on ebony wing

Harbinger of night

Love's Trilogy

Rendezvous

Driven by passion

Lovers pledge fidelity

A kiss seals the troth

Recrimination

Anger burns the soul

Painful words long remembered

Forgiveness denied

Epitaph

On the grave stone carved

"When it's over, it's over"

In love, as in life

April

Soft warmth surrounding

Playful wind whirling raindrops

Scattering petals

January 1, 2003

TANKA   (Haiku variation 5-7-5-7-7 syllable pattern)

December

Deer in the ravine

Snowflakes sifting, drifting down

Winter's confection

Adorns evergreen branches

North wind a will-o'-the-wisp

December 9, 2002

Spring Song

Tulip magnolia

Encircled by daffodils

Splash of golden sun

Sighing softly, passing breeze

Kisses spring's fleeting array

April 15, 2005

Snow Drops

Green leaves spearing snow

Blossoms nod and bow their heads

Tossed by wintr'y winds

April 10, 2003

Sunbeam

The promise of light

Glowing, dancing, dawn to dark

Vibrant life renewed

May 22, 2003

Sentinel Oak

Lonely skeleton

Bereft, your leaves gone missing

Keep watch through the days

November 13, 2003

Japan

Islands in the sea

Mountains peeking through the mist

All is calm, serene

January 29, 2004

(printed and distributed as example of Haiku for facilitators at the Chicago Botanic Garden 5th/6th grade classes - Sansho En - winter and spring 2004)

Japanese Garden

Patterns traced in sand

Sometimes curving, sometimes straight

Symbols, age and peace

February 27, 2004

Cardinal in Winter

Scarlet cardinal

Take shelter in the pine boughs

As snowflakes whisper

March 9, 2004

Bumblebee Morning

Pollen gatherer

Stops at bluebell trumpets sweet

Her baskets to fill

Bumblebee Evening

Amid trumpets blue

Black head searching, wings now stilled

Pollen baskets filled

April 29, 2004

Autumn

Maple leaf carpet

Scarlet, golden warp and woof

Covers forest floor.

September 17, 2004

Farewell to Summer

Wavelets kiss the shore

Seagulls bob on gentle swells

Summer's last refrain.

September 21, 2004   (seen at Lake Michigan)

Autumn Tableau

Autumn patchwork quilt

Scarlet maple, golden birch

Stitched by evergreen

October 15, 2004 (observed on trip to Minnesota)

Marco Evening

Cerulean sea

Softly kiss spun sugar sand

Palm frond lullaby

January 27, 2005   (Florida vacation)

Butler Park Pond

Proudly black geese stroll

Across pond ice capped by snow

Webbed prints mark the path

February 10, 2005   (Daniel's drama class)

Spring Song

River's captive ice

Groaning, cracking, breaking free

Winter's last refrain

March 11, 2005   (Chicago Botanic Garden)

Guardian Wolf

Atop the far ridge

Solitary sentinel

Lonely vigil keeps

March 26, 2005

April

Sky awash with blue

Dancing diamonds waltz on waves

Swans and cygnets glide

April 2, 2005   (Chicago Botanic Garden)

Ancient Oak

Oak from ancient days

Only skeleton remains

Pointing to the clouds

May 24, 2005 (ravine at Rosewood Beach)

Mayapple

Mayapple blossom

Sheltered by parasols green

Chipmunk hidey-hole

May 24, 2005 (ravine path at Rosewood Beach)

Hibiscus

Hibiscus blossom

Coral petals veined with rose

Only for a day

June 6, 2005

Arkansas Dawn

Mysterious mist

White cloud drifts down mountainside

Rests on azure lake

June 7, 2005 (a memory from 1991 trip)

Egret

Egret's reflection

Mirrored, moving through the pond

On a summer's eve

June 7, 2005

Summer Shower

Quilted clouds of gray

Flirting with a sky of bluesummer's face

Sun plays hide and seek.

June 14, 2005

Playful Breeze

Breeze tickles treetops

Tosses branches playfully

Rocking nesting birds.

June 1, 2005   (Cathy's back yard)

Summer's Face

Summer's face revealed.

Chicory and Queen Ann's lace

By a dusty road

June 24, 2005 – Happy Birthday, Daniel!

Monday at the Botanic Garden

Softly comes twilight

Carillon melodies ring

Red wing trills his note

July 11, 2005

Seagull Respite

Seagulls take their ease

Perched atop the long sea wall

Facing evening's breeze

September 6, 2005

Winter Frost

Filigree of lace

Frozen on the windowpanes

Heavy hangs the day

September 6, 2005

Premonition

Winter's frosty breath

North Wind stirring slate gray clouds

On Autumn's doorstep

September 16, 2005

Deer Path

Deep down the ravine

Oak leaves strewn across the path

Crunch beneath deer hoofs

November 7, 2005

Bird Gleaners

Busy bird gleaners

Sparrows peck at peanut bits

Left by scolding jays

November 16, 2005

Winter Overture

Pristine snowflakes fly

Driven by relentless wind

Winter Overture

November 16, 2005

Goddess of the Night

Veiled by a thin cloud

The full moon gazes earthward

Goddess of the night

April 11, 2006

Fireflies

Blinking in the night

Fireflies lift their lanterns high

Lighting the way home

July 3, 2006

September Song

Northeast wind a-blow

Curling waves crash on the shore

Seagulls hug the pier

September 1, 2006

Sunset at Lake Michigan

Lavender sunset

East breeze beckons waves ashore

Twilight slips away

Purple shadows hail the moon

Filled with gold she surfs the clouds

September 7, 2006

Ravine Patterns

Patterns high above

Oak leaves stenciled on the clouds

Painted by the wind

July 15, 2009

Lake Michigan

Strata in the lake

Cobalt on the horizon

Turquoise by the shore

September 2009

Jack in the Pulpit   (tanka)

Jack in the Pulpit

Proudly you preached in springtime

Red berries remain

Where once you stood resplendent

North winds howl and snow resides

September 14, 2009

Outer Banks   (tanka)

Curling, crashing waves

Flinging salt-laced foam ashore

Pelicans glide, dive

Sandpipers and Kittiwakes

Leave webbed imprints in damp sand

Kill Devil Hills - September 17, 2009

Winter Photo

Sunlight marks a path

Across ice covered lagoon

Snow drifts hug the shore

January 19, 2010 – Chicago Botanic Garden

Sansho En

As afternoon wanes

Pine trees cast slate blue shadows

Against pristine snow

January 19, 2010 – Chicago Botanic Garden

Backyard Portrait   **tanka – a variation of haiku – 5-7-5-7-7 syllables**

A freshening breeze

Stirs ripples in the bird bath

A deer stops to drink

Blue jay bandits steal peanuts

While squirrels complain and scold

April 2010

Swans

Ripples in the pond

Become "V's" then disappear

Swans silently glide

April 2010

Rosewood Beach

Waves assault the pier

Slap concrete pilings then break

On the rock strewn shore

March 2010

Weeping Willow

Trailing long tresses

Willow weeps beside the pond

Grief's sorrowful muse

June 22, 2010   Happy Birthday, Bob and Beck!

Sheridan Road

Behind the guard rail

Yellow blossoms bend and bow

Greeting passersby

July 19, 2010

Broken Oak   (tanka)

Trunk of broken oak

Spans the creek in the ravine

Challenge unspoken

Chipmunks race with abandon

Across the new wooden bridge

July 19, 2010

Lake Michigan Afternoon   (tanka)

Seagull rides the buoy

Wings unfurled, he gently bobs

As waves pass beneath

Leave foam ashore then retreat

The warm sand sighs with relief

July 19, 2010

God's Cathedral (tanka)

In God's cathedral

Leafless branches arch the path

In silent prayer

Winter song a hymn of praise

As snow blankets the altar

September 12, 2010

Vigil (tanka)

Fields sere and golden

Corn and soybeans harvested

To begin new life

They'll keep their lonely vigil

Awaiting the warm spring rains   **(driving to North Woods 9/17/10)**

Lumberjacks Camp (tanka)

Cold September morn

En route to Logging Camp 5

Old steam engine chuffs

Trailing smoke amid the pines

Lumberjacks no longer come

September 18, 2010 – Laona, Wisconsin

Project Linus – **2011 Winner at Annual Tea**

Blankets made with love

All aboard the dream-time train

In the Land of Nod

October Evening

Breath of southeast wind

Gently coaxes waves ashore

Touches trembling trees

October 17, 2011

Summer Morning

Spanking northeast breeze

Dark waves gather in the lake

Crest and race ashore

June 25, 2012

Storm

Bent, bowed, unbroken

Still reaching for the heavens

Through the storm of life

January 19, 2013

Mystic trees

how can you not know

spirits dwell within the trees

they whisper your name

June 23, 2013

mem'ries of childhood

damp footprints across warm sand

in search of beach glass

July 31, 2013

swirls across the snow

carved, abandoned by the wind

await renewal

a landscape as yet undreamed

by an unseen architect

June 27, 2013

maple flags unfurled

dancing to a northeast tune

as autumn returns

September 30, 2013

whitecaps gently break

clouds piled against horizon

leaves drift lazily

piers abandoned by seagulls

egret lonely sentinel

October 7, 2013

Abrupt Winter

leaves suddenly gone

ruby crab apples appear

a winter necklace

sparkling among the branches

delight of bird jewel thieves

November 15, 2013

Night

black velvet curtain

pinned in place by silver stars

quintessential night

February 29, 2016

2nd place winner, resident – Highland Park Poetry - 2016

Broken Horse

bronze large narrow horse

your poor broken leg won't heal

steel horses gallop

their wheels creating chaos

yet you elicit a smile

August 1, 2017

one of multiple winners – HP Poetry contest

for art and sculpture pieces in parks in HP

to be placed on a sign by the horse at the

Ravinia train station from the middle of

September until December

Autumn Tapestry (haiku)

autumn tapestry

scarlet maple, golden birch

stitched by evergreen

Illinois Tanka

voices from the past

pleading, hoping to be free

Lincoln's legacy

emancipation proclaimed

avatar for the ages

Song of the Shore

Tracing the shore by the restless sea
earth beckons with infinite peace.
Sea oats wave gently as gulls glide and turn
while the ebb and the flow seek release.

Across the mud flats tiny feet leave their patterns
where mussels abandon their shells.
Seaweed and driftwood are swirled and delivered,
the cadence and coda of swells.

Offshore lie the ribs of a skeleton ship
run aground on a devious sandbar.
At the delta's wide sweep the river seeks union
as evening returns by the light of a star.

Winner – 2015 Poetry That Moves – May 2015

Love

Who is it that I see when I look in your eyes?

I see the soul of God clothed in little boy disguise.

I know you.

I've known you many times before in other days and places.

You've taken different forms, it's true, worn many different faces,

but I know you.

Sometimes I may forget your truth or may not understand

until you reach out, gently, and take me by the hand;

then I know you.

No matter where we wander – beyond all worlds, all time –

our hearts entrain in peace and love, our thoughts in perfect rhyme.

Yes. I know you.

Broken Horse

Bronze large narrow horse

Your poor broken leg won't heal

Steel horses gallop

Their wheels creating chaos

Yet you elicit a smile

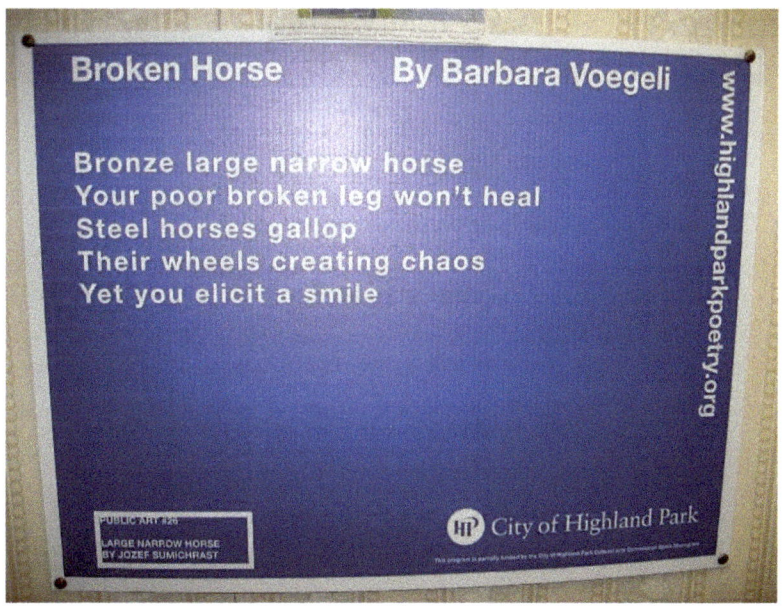

Snowdrops

Tender leaves spear snow

Blossoms nod and bow their heads

Tossed by wintry winds

Fireflies

<u>December</u>   Tanka – Haiku variation 5-7-5-7- 7 syllable pattern

Deer in the ravine

Snowflakes sifting, drifting down

Winter's confection

Adorns evergreen branches

North Wind a will-o'-the-wisp

Sculpture

giant butterfly

forged in fire to hardened steel

never to take flight

to sip sweet nectar - to dream

forever tethered to earth

Spring Fanfare

Daffodil trumpets

Forsythia bells of gold

Easter musicale

Lake Michigan Sunset

Lavender sunset

East breeze beckons waves ashore

Twilight slips away

Purple shadows hail the moon

Filled with gold she surfs the clouds

Autumn Tableau

Autumn patchwork quilt

Scarlet maple, golden birch

Stitched by evergreen

Winter Cathedral

In God's cathedral

Leafless branches arch the path

And pray in silence

Winter hymn a song of praise

As snow blankets the altar

Haiku: Traditional

winter's frosty breath

north wind a will-o'-the-wisp

on autumn's doorstep

RAINBOW IN MY WEB

There's a rainbow in my web today, said Spider to the sun.

    I saw it there at break of day when the spinning work was done.

I fashioned the web with strings of pearls that sparkle with the dew,

    In lovely iridescent shades of green and pink and blue.

The gossamer strands, so lovingly spun, were caught by a passing breeze

    Whose gentle fingers plucked the harp in fanciful harmonies.

The rainbow disappeared too soon with the fading of the light,

    To reappear when moonbeams came to dance all through the night.

I Know You

Who is it that I see

        When I look in your eyes?

I see the soul of God

        Clothed in little boy disguise.

        I know you

Sometimes I may forget your truth

        Or may not understand

Until you reach out, sweetly,

        And take me by the hand.

        Then I know you

I've known you many times before

        In other days and places.

You've taken different forms, it's true

        Worn many different faces.

But I know you

No matter where we wander

    Beyond all worlds, all time,

Our hearts entrain in peace and love,

    Our thoughts in perfect rhyme.

    Oh, yes, I know you

Though your lips may never speak my name

    Your eyes tell me so much.

Such beauty dwells within your heart,

    Such warmth is in your touch.

    You are love

To Bobby   8/31/1999

Agape

Who is it that I see when I look into your eyes?

I see the soul of God clothed in little boy disguise.

I know you.

I've known you many times before in other days and places.

You've taken different forms, it's true, worn many different faces,

but I know you.

Sometimes I may forget your truth or may not understand

until you reach out, gently, and take me by the hand;

then I know you.

No matter where we wander - beyond all worlds, all time -

our hearts entrain in peace and love, our thoughts in perfect rhyme.

Yes, I know you.

Although you cannot speak my name your eyes tell me so much.

Undying love spills from your heart and warms me when we touch.

I know you - and you know me.

revised April 2013

TRANSCENDENCE

The journey's long and treacherous, the road ahead unclear.

Time is now the enemy, though it isn't death I fear.

Sorrow and longing mark the hours with overwhelming pain.

The sun is lost behind dark clouds. No light will come again.

The heartless days my soul entrap; I cannot see an ending.

Black-bordered nights assail me now, the rage and tears, all blending.

Despair surrounds each moment here. To die would be such bliss.

There must be hope within my heart. My love, send me a kiss!

You cannot send a kiss or word. I know that this is true,

But I hold fast and cherish, still, sweet memories of you.

Why do we cry when hope is gone, there's nothing else remains?

When all is lost, the truth is this – 'tis only love sustains.

February 2000

KARMA

Here beneath the starlit sky

    Alone, but for the moon, I lie

And ponder, as the stars swirl by –

    Where leads my path? And why?

May 1994

Ballad of the Bugs

Ha-ha-ha! Hee-hee-hee!

Here come the tickle bugs,

One, two, three!

Ha-ha-ha! Hee-hee-hee!

Here come the giggle bugs.

Giggle along with me!

Ha-ha-ha! Hee-hee-hee!

Here come the doodle bugs.

Fiddle-dee, fiddle-dee-dee!

Ha-ha-ha! Hee-hee-hee!

Here's comes a ladybug Crawling on my knee!

Ha-ha-ha! Hee-hee-hee!

Something's sitting on my nose.

I hope it's not a bee!

Ha-ha-ha! Hee-hee-hee!

All the bugs have flown away.

Will you come play with me?

Bobby, my giggle bug
Becky, my tickle bug
Daniel, my doodle bug

Love, Beah   April 18, 2002

SHE FELL IN THE VAT OF MOLASSES

She fell in the vat.
        She stepped on the cat?
O, no, Rebecca would never do that!
        She fell in the vat of molasses.

My, it's sticky in there!
        Is there gum in her hair?
O, no, Rebecca would certainly not care,
        But her headband is in the molasses.

It was difficult to swim.
        Perhaps it was a whim,
But Rebecca was so full of vigor and vim
        That she dog paddled through the molasses.

She forgot her swimsuit?
        Yes, Rebecca's so cute.
And a backstroke so strong it was really a beaut,
        She finally escaped the molasses.

She won't fall this time.

    Look, she stopped on a dime!

For Rebecca and me it's the end of the rhyme,

    'Cause she dived in the vat of molasses!

To Rebecca with hugs and giggles   *Love, BaBa*   July 12, 2001*

* Becky's current name for me

PORTRAIT OF MARCH

Daffodils nod their golden heads.

Kites dance above with the wind.

Icicles melt in the warmth of the sun –

Old Winter his time must rescind.

Forsythia branches are bending with bloom.

Birdsong breaks forth in a rush.

Springtime's bare canvas is painted afresh

With Nature's magnanimous brush.

February 21, 2001

THE MERMAID

The mermaid swims beneath the sea

Among the starfish, wild and free.

Her only wish a fanciful life

Above the sea, as the Captain's wife.

Composed and sent by email to Becky   February 21, 2001

To: Becky, Bobby, Daniel

From: Beah

Dear Becky, Bobby, and Daniel,

Spring is coming soon, I hear.
Who told me that? The little bear.
He just awoke from his winter nap
And came to snuggle on my lap.

My lap is usually reserved for three
Of the dearest children, as you can see.
I told him that he mustn't stay,
So he blew me a kiss as he ran away.
Mama bear waited to take his paw.
It was the dearest thing I ever saw!
Little Bear turned with a friendly wave
Then disappeared inside his cave.

He wanted to wish all of you Happy Spring,

And before I sign off there is just one more thing.

I love you to pieces, but that's nothing new.

Springtime or anytime, that's truer than true.

Hugs and kisses,

Beah   February 23, 2001

THE ROSE

Donnie Voegeli

(1964 – 1991)

It began as a tiny bud, the promise of its

    beauty and delicate fragrance

    hidden within tender young leaves

    that enfolded and protected its essence.

Kissed by rain in the springtime of its life,

    the rose felt the stirrings of its purpose;

    reaching toward the warmth and light,

    the petals opened in answer to its song.

Drawn by its perfume, passersby paused

    to search for the source;

    enchanted by its radiance, they caressed

    soft velvet and were blessed.

In innocence the rose existed

  for the sheer joy of existence,

 unmindful of the benediction it

  bestowed on all it touched.

With grace and beauty by love disposed

 it followed its destiny, petal and thorn.

In predawn stillness the gardener came

 to gather the rose, though not full-blown.

Teardrops of dew clung fast to the leaves

 and half-opened petals of scarlet hue.

With loving care the gardener smiled

 then pressed the rose to his heart

SONG OF THE SHORE

Tracing the shore by the restless sea

earth beckons with infinite peace.

Sea oats wave gently as gulls glide and turn

while the ebb and flow seek release.

Across the mud flats tiny feet leave their patterns

where mussels abandon their shells.

Seaweed and driftwood are swirled and delivered,

the cadence and coda of swells.

Offshore lie the ribs of a skeleton ship

Run aground on a treacherous sandbar.

At the delta the river seeks union with sea

As homeward I turn by the light of a star.

JOURNEY'S END

Ahead the endless journey lies.

    How far away the bridge!

Beyond the farthest mountain

    where horizon meets the ridge.

How very low the spirit.

    How deep and dark its dwelling.

The loneliness and heartbreak

    an abyss beyond the telling.

So cruel the pain within my soul,

    the days and nights forlorn.

Until we meet on rainbow's bridge

    to life, and love, reborn.

Star Path

I wish you safe journey though near or afar.

A trip 'round the corner, a flight to a star.

A hand joined in friendship, a prayer on the wind
        For bittersweet closure, new life to begin.

I wish you red roses whose petals won't fade,

        To bloom in your heart with our love, there portrayed.

I'm still there beside you, I didn't go far -

        Around the next corner and east of a star.

February 2003   For Carol on the loss of Bob

For Wilma - Sept. 7, 2003

For Marge and "Bum" Baraconi - July 25, 2012

ROUND IS THE SUN

Round is the sun, golden bright in the sky.

    Round is the shape of a squishy mud pie.

Round is the clock. Hear it tick tock the time.

    Round is a penny. Round is a dime.

Round is a cupcake, all chocolate and yummy.

    Round is a gumball, all chewy and gummy.

Round are the wheels of my steam engine train.

    Round are the wheels of a school bus, a plane.

Round is a ball. We can bounce and play catch.

    Round is a cookie. Let's bake another batch!

Round is a ferris wheel turning so high

    That I can reach way up and touch the blue sky.

Round goes the carousel. Horses we'll ride!

    To magical music they prance, side by side.

Round is the tummy of my teddy bear friend.

    He smiles when I hug him, he tickles my chin.

Round is the moon spilling silvery light.

    Round is a hug and a warm kiss good night.

September 2002

You Are My Sunshine

I like to swing and swig a pop.

I like to jump and never stop.

From swing to trampoline I run

So outdoor play is twice the fun.

I bounce on butt, I fall to knees

Then stand and jump as high as the trees.

Now it's back to have a tummy swing,

And Mama's here - so I play the king.

She always knows just what's in store
As, hands together, I signal "more."
Nudie Boy gives her a merry chase,

With eyes alight and a smile on my face.

When she runs and catches me,

Her answering smile of love I see.

Whatever I do and wherever I run,

Her love is as bright as the summer sun.

        I love you, Mama.

            Bobby

"He's a good boy to his Mama."

          July 7, 2003

The Fairy Queen

In a faraway valley with a rippling rill

A fairy queen ruled her kingdom with a will.

Rebecca Ann was the queen's given name,

And far and away was the reach of her fame.

She was blond and beautiful, a mere slip of a girl

With eyes of pale green and fair skin like a pearl.

Fairies have wings, and, of course, they can fly

Across the wide valley to mountaintops high.

A fairy has magic, and the queen most of all,

So Rebecca declared there should be a grand ball.

A courier was summoned and sent through the land

To invite all the fairies to the ball she had planned.

The Fairy of Music soon answered the call,

For what is a party without music, after all?

Fairy pipers and harpists, violinists as well,

Took wing down the mountain and over the dell.

A fine fairy orchestra played in the hall

As the Fairy of Dance arrived at the ball.

She brought all her minions to dance the gavotte,

Then twirled 'round the floor and performed the fox trot.

The Fairy of Flowers caused orchids to bloom

On crystal chandeliers that hung in the room.

Next came the Fairy of Merriment and Laughter

Who promised a night to remember ever after.

In a manner so courtly, one now seldom seen,

The Fairy of Light bowed low before the queen.

Rebecca joined hands with the Fairy of Light,

And they danced and they laughed through the magical night.

It happened long ago, but the fairies still recall

The night when their queen was the belle of the ball.

Stars winked against velvet in the night sky above,

And Rebecca was known as the Fairy of Love.

She married her prince – she had found Mister Right,

And they ruled their fair kingdom with love and with light.

    For Becky   October 31, 2003

Winter's Tale

Landscape drawn by snowflakes white

Sifting, drifting through the night.

Whipped cream frosting piled on posts,

Snowmen posing, wint'ry ghosts.

Winter's tale once more retold

Swirling snowflakes, north wind cold.

January 27, 2004

sent by email to Bobby, Becky and Daniel

Robins in the Maple Tree

There's a robin's nest upon my branch said maple to the oak.

Mama and Papa built the nest, and it's filled with feathery folk.

Mama Robin keeps them warm while Papa looks for food.

It takes a lot of bugs and worms to feed the hungry brood!

Sometimes Papa babysits while Mama finds a meal,

So someone's always near the nest; now that's the robins' deal!

Baby birds are growing fast, and soon they'll leave the nest.

Now it's time to see which baby robin flies the best.

They flap their tiny wings and jump then spiral round and round,

Until their little robin feet are safely on the ground.

When cool winds blow and autumn comes, "Good-bye the robins sing.

We'll spend the winter where it's warm and see you in the spring!"

February 15, 2004

A Spider Danced

A spider danced across her web one bright and sunny day.

"Hello!" she called to a passing fly. "Will you please come and play?"

    The fly went on his way.

Honeybee came buzzing by in search of fragrant flowers.

She said, "I've lots of work to do. Can't waste these golden hours."

    Bee left for distant bowers.

Worker ants beneath the web saw spider way up high.

"A cup of coffee?" spider said. "Perhaps a piece of pie?"

    Ants marched right on by.

Ladybug flew by the brook to have a nice, cool drink.

"Let's have cake," the spider said, "with lemonade, all pink."

    Lady refused, I think.

Dragonfly came darting by, a tasty snack to find.

"Stop and visit," spider said, "if you would be so kind."

    Dragonfly paid no mind.

Spider sighed. "I'm all alone. There's nothing more to say."

Just then her egg case opened. Baby spiders saved the day.

    Three cheers! Hip, hip, hooray!

August 2, 2004

Sir Lancelot's Debut

In days of yore Sir Lancelot

  Was given to sing and dance a lot

    Until one fine day

      He danced a ballet

        Then folk looked at him askance a lot

Scarlet

Scarlet

Dramatic, fiery

Pulsating, radiating, exploding

Leaps from palette to creation

Crimson

1st Prize Cinquains/Highland Park Resident - Poetry Challenge – April 2014

Honorable Mention in Colors/Highland Park Resident

To Becky on the occasion of her brilliant performance as Marcy Park

"The 25th Annual Putnam County Spelling Bee"

Libertyville Civic Center

August, 2010

Congratulations, Miss Marcy Park!

It was a great performance, and what a lark!

We loved your totally terrific tumbling,

And seeing Jesus was truly humbling.

Your singing, your chutzpah – what more can I say?

Being there onstage with you sure made my day.

So here's to the future – that's no shot in the dark:

No pun intended, you knocked it out of the park!

Star of the Week

I have a problem. My stomach is turning cartwheels, and I guess it shows. On the drive to school, Mom looks at me in the rearview mirror. "You don't look happy, Becky. I thought you liked first grade."

"It's my turn to be star of the week," I say glumly.

"I know," says Mom. "You did a great job arranging and taping your gymnastics photos to your poster."

I sigh. "Making the poster was the easy part. Now I have to stand up in front of the class and tell them about the pictures."

Mom nods. "That can be scary. If you talk about how much fun gymnastics is, you'll forget about being afraid."

"I get all tongue tied when I have to talk in class. Yesterday I got the wrong answer in math, and a couple of the kids laughed at me. Then when we were on the playground at recess, Marissa said I was dumb. I couldn't think of anything mean to say, so I just walked away."

Mom parks in front of Rockland Elementary. "Walking away was hard to do," she says. "Sometimes what you do is just as important as what you say. I'm proud of you, Becky."

I get out of the car, grab the poster and close the door. "You think everything I do is great. That's because you're my mom."

Mom reaches through the open window and touches my cheek. "No matter what, you'll always be my shining star," she says. "Now give me a smile before you go." Mom pretends to frown. "This is the smile police speaking."

I giggle. "Okay, smile police." As Mom drives away I slowly walk to the classroom. Arms crossed, Marissa waits inside the door.

"Here's our little star," she smirks as she grabs the poster.

Miss Chase, our teacher, walks across the room. "Good morning, Becky. Marissa, give Becky the poster so she can put it by the blackboard for everyone to see." With a scowl on her face, Marissa obeys.

Miss Chase smiles at me. "I'll round up the children."

Chewing my bottom lip, I stand at the blackboard. Legs crossed, the kids sit on the rug and stare. And stare. My heart races and my stomach does flip-flops.

"As you know," Miss Chase says, "Becky is our star of the week. Tell us about the pictures on your poster, Becky."

Marissa makes a silly face at me. I open my mouth, but my tongue is glued to the roof of my mouth. It's like having a mouth full of peanut butter. As if that's not bad enough, Marissa sticks out her tongue.

"What's the matter?" Marissa asks. "Cat got your tongue?"

Everyone laughs. "Marissa!" Miss Chase scolds.

Twisting a strand of hair around my finger, I rock from one foot to the other. Why didn't I tell Mom I was sick so I could stay home? I can't think of a thing to say. I want to run out the door. Instead, I drop to my knees and do forward rolls across the room.

"Wow!" says one of the boys.

I cartwheel back across the room as all the kids clap. With a skip and a hop, I put my hands on the floor and reach for the ceiling with my feet. I hold the pose as long as I can then right myself. "That was a hand stand," I say."

The kids jump up and crowd around my poster. They point to the pictures, and my tongue works just fine as I tell them how much fun gymnastics is. After a few minutes Miss Chase thanks me and says it's time to work. As the kids walk away, I feel a tap on my shoulder. I turn around and see Marissa.

"That was really cool," she says. "Could you teach me how to do a cartwheel?"

I think about walking away, but I decide it's time for words. "Yesterday you said I was dumb. If I'm so dumb, how can I teach you anything?"

Marissa looks down at her feet. "I'm sorry," she says. "It was a dumb thing to say, so I guess that makes me the one who's dumb."

"Gymnastics is fun, but it takes hard work and lots of practice," I tell her. "If you really want to, I could give you a lesson at recess."

Marissa grins and curls her little finger around mine. "Pinky promise?" she says.

"Pinky promise," I repeat.

Marissa links arms with me. "I can't wait for recess," she says.

THEATER ON THE LAKE

The opening curtain slowly parts

  humid air pulses with an ominous rhythm

    soft breeze lifts branches, stirs leaves

      empty chairs, apprehensive, wait and watch

        the overture begins quietly then builds

Clouds of slate edged with black

  lend a heightened sense of foreboding

    dark props line a stage with no actors

      a playbill devoid of ads and cast members

        no listing or history of previous roles

Breeze becomes wind; a distant sound rumbles

  orchestra plays from a discordant score

    angry clouds roil and race in a game of tag

      cymbals crash and drumbeats pound

        klieg lights, hot and blinding

          flash on and off

Shrieking wind whips trees, snaps branches

   flinging rain and tossing hailstones

      a wild pas de deux of timbre and tempo

         chairs join the dance, twirl and overturn

            tent flaps snap free and whine manic tunes

Tension builds to crescendo, finds sudden release

  as wind chases dark clouds across the lake

     thunder cracks then flees to rumble in the distance

      raindrops beat a soft staccato as unseen hands

        drop the curtain on the matinee performance

tea, anyone?

tea

party

White Rabbit

the Mad Hatter

and Alice, of course

cucumber sandwiches

custard tarts topped by whipped cream

blueberry scones with lemon curd

but I declined the invitation

my favorite fare is pizza and beer

This creative poem was used as a teaching example and in its presentation in the shape of a tea cup.

The Little Christmas Tree in the Forest

Standing in a clearing, the little cedar tree shivered as the December wind whistled a ragged tune through his branches. It seemed only yesterday that warm breezes had feathered through his needles, playfully tossing the slender branches to and fro. How he missed the robins that had built their nest in his branches!

Every day for weeks the parent birds searched for juicy berries and fat worms to feed their four babies. In the evenings when the baby birds' tummies were full, the warm southern breeze hummed a lullaby. Moving his branches gently back and forth, the little tree rocked the baby robins and their exhausted parents to sleep.

When summer ended, the oaks dropped their acorns and then their leaves. It was time to fly south for the winter, so the robins took wing. "Good-bye," they said. "We'll be back in the spring." That had been weeks ago, and the little tree felt cold and lonely.

Sounds of people broke the silence. As the sounds came closer, the little tree spoke to the wise old balsam that grew nearby. "Why are people in the forest on such a cold day?" The balsam shook his branches slowly but did not answer.

Day after day the little cedar heard people, but he could not see them. The cardinals visited every day looking for seeds. When the sounds of people came near, they flew away. The chickadee followed high above the treetops calling his name as he flew. "Dee-dee-dee! Chick-a-dee-dee-dee!" Squirrels scampered up the oak trees to leafy nests high above the floor of the forest. Deer ran for the safety of the thicket.

One day people came to the clearing. They cut down the evergreen trees with axes. The Scotch pines were cut and dragged away, then the firs and finally the balsams. The old balsam shook as the blows of the ax made deep slashes in its trunk. The little tree was so frightened that he shook from his topmost branch to his roots.

"Stop!" he begged. "Why are they doing this? I thought only big trees were used for lumber. You are old but not so big that your wood amounts to anything." With a final blow of the ax, the old balsam swayed and toppled on its side. The little cedar watched as his old neighbor was dragged away and disappeared over the hill. As the last bit of sunlight slipped beyond the hills darkness fell across the clearing. The little tree shuddered. He had never been so alone.

Next morning the gray squirrel ran down the oak at the edge of the clearing. He jumped near the little tree and pushed aside the fallen leaves. Using his sharp claws, gray squirrel dug in the ground. "For goodness sakes!" he fussed. "Why do I go through this every year? I know my acorns are here somewhere, but I can never remember just where I put them."

The little tree shook with laughter. "How do you find enough to eat to keep body and squirrel together? I have never seen anyone so absent minded in all my life!"

Gray squirrel raised his head and glared. "Is that so?" he said. "In all your life, you say. As if you've seen a dozen winters come and go! I remember when you were nothing more than a sapling last year. I suppose I do look a little silly poking my nose under every leaf in the forest, but some of us have to work for a living. Not like those who just stand around all day and night."

The little tree nodded. "You're right," he agreed. "I apologize. Can you tell me the meaning of the strange happenings in the forest?"

"What's this about strange happenings?" asked Gray Squirrel.

"For days now people have been in the forest cutting down trees with their axes. Night falls and all is peaceful, but when morning comes, it starts all over again. I'm afraid that I may be next."

Gray Squirrel nodded. "I heard the people, too. I am afraid of men and hide whenever they are in the forest, but I'm also as curious as those peculiar creatures called

cats. When the cutting noises stopped one day last week, I poked my head out of my nest

and looked around. Two men from the Bowman farm loaded cut trees on a large

wooden sled hitched to two horses. When the men finished cutting trees, they led the horses away. I followed the sled until it disappeared over sunset hill. From the top of the hill I watched the men drive the horses across the field. They took the trees into the barn and closed the barn doors."

"How brave you are!" said the little cedar.

"Not really," chuckled Gray Squirrel. "Just curious, as I said before." His eyes danced with excitement. "One of the men came out of the barn carrying a tree and took it inside the farmhouse."

The little cedar leaned forward eagerly. "What happened then?" he asked.

"I waited at the edge of the farmyard for a long time," said Gray Squirrel. "I had to know why anyone would take a tree inside a house."

The little cedar shook his branches. "What strange creatures people are," he said.

"I agree," answered Gray Squirrel. "When I could stand the mystery no longer, I hopped across the yard. I stopped every three or four hops to look around and sniff the air for danger. I saw a bird feeder hanging on a limb close to a window, so I climbed the tree and slowly moved down the limb. When I jumped on the feeder, it bounced so much that it made me dizzy."

The little tree chuckled. "Could you see inside the house?" he asked.

Gray Squirrel nodded. "You'll never believe what I saw through the farmhouse window."

"Oh, tell me," begged the little cedar.

"The tree was standing upright in front of the window," said Gray Squirrel. "It looked as if it were still growing in the forest and had never felt the blade of an ax."

The little tree gasped. "Why in the world would people cut a tree and leave it inside a house?" he asked.

"Beats me," said Gray Squirrel. "There were bright, shiny things hanging from every branch, and colored lights had been strung from top to bottom. At the very top of the tree was a big star. And on the floor underneath the tree were boxes of all sizes wrapped in colored papers and tied with beautiful ribbons. It was the most amazing thing I've ever seen!"

Toogie and Bob

Bob was tired at the end of the day. Ever since sunrise the little engine had been running back and forth along the track from the Thompson Quarry to the harbor. Pulling cars loaded with the heavy stones from the quarry was hard work. Bob was happy when the last car was uncoupled. Now he'd have time to say hello to Toogie, his little tugboat friend. Toogie was already tied up for the night at the pier. "Toot toot!" whistled Bob. Toogie answered with two little blasts of his horn. "Boop boop!"

"It was a hard day," said Bob. "I'm ready for my shed. How are you?" he asked his friend.

"Tired," said Toogie. "I've been pushing barges out of the harbor all day. The barges get angry when I push them, but that's the only way I can move them to the breakwater. I'm always glad to see the big tugboats come to take the barges downriver." Toogie sighed. "My job is not fun."

"Neither is mine," Bob said. "The cars complained that they were too heavy when we left the quarry. They grumbled all the way to the docks. After the dockworkers unloaded the stones, the empty cars were so much easier to pull, but they were still cross. They accused me of racing because we got back to the quarry in lickety-split time. Mr. Thompson told me that I'm too little for this job, so I've been trying to go faster. I'm worried that he may send me away."

"That would be terrible," said Toogie. "You're my friend. Talking to you always makes me feel better, no matter how badly the barges have behaved all day."

"Thank you, Toogie," said Bob. "You always make me feel better, too." Bob's wheels began to turn. "Good night and pleasant dreams," he said as he puffed away.

It was a long time before Toogie slept. He couldn't imagine life at the harbor without Bob. He decided not to think about it anymore and finally fell asleep.

The next day Toogie spent all morning pushing the balky barges across the harbor. It was afternoon before he realized that he hadn't seen Bob. I hope Bob didn't have a breakdown, Toogie thought. He worked hard all afternoon, but there was no sign of Bob. Finally Toogie pushed the last barge to the breakwater where a big tugboat was waiting.

With the day's work done Toogie rested by the pier. He still hadn't seen Bob or heard his whistle. When night came Toogie began to worry again. What if Mr. Thompson had taken Bob off the quarry line?

What if he had decided to sell Bob to another railroad? Either way Toogie would never see his friend again. Toogie felt so lonesome that his eyes filled with tears.

By the time the sun came up Toogie was already hard at work. The barges fussed and complained as he pushed them across the harbor. Toogie felt sad as he started back to the docks, but the sound of a familiar whistle lifted his spirits. "Toot toot, toot toot," Bob signaled his friend as he stopped near the pier.

"Boop boop, boop boop!" Toogie's horn blasted happily. He was so excited that he almost skipped across the waves. "Bob," he said. "I'm so glad you're here. I didn't think I'd ever see you again."

"It's good to see you, Toogie," Bob said. "Mr. Thompson is sending me away, but it's going to be all right. He owns the kiddy park in town. There's a track that runs all around the park, and he's asked me to pull the cars filled with children. Won't that be fun?" Bob asked.

"Yes," Toogie agreed. "I'm very happy that you'll have such a good life, but I'll miss seeing you and talking to you."

"I have a surprise for you," Bob said. "Do you see this flatcar that I'm pulling? I have a special reason for bringing it today. It's for you."

"For me? How can it be for me?" asked Toogie. "I'm only good for pushing barges. I can't push a flatcar. Besides, a flatcar won't float."

"You're right," laughed Bob, "but you'll float. There's a lake at the kiddy park, and Mr. Thompson wants you to give the children boat rides around the lake every day. That's why I brought the flatcar. Once you're aboard I can take you to the park. Mr. Thompson wants us to have a new home there."

"Yippee," shouted Toogie. He was so excited he couldn't stop blowing his horn and making circles in the water.

"Mr. Thompson built a brand new shed for me," Bob said, "and you have your very own boathouse nearby. Taking the children for rides will be fun. We won't hear anymore grumbling cars or complaining barges. We'll hear laughter and all the happy sounds of children having a good time."

"We'll have a good time, too," Toogie told Bob. "Ready when you are!"

Bob backed the flatcar to the pier as the harbor crane lifted Toogie out of the water. When Toogie was resting safely on the flatcar, Bob tooted his whistle. "All aboard, Toogie!" Wheels turning and whistle blowing, Bob sped away. He and Toogie were on the way to Mr. Thompson's kiddy park and their new life filled with fun and friendship.

WE'RE ALL WINNERS

A brisk wind snapped the Illinois and American flags at the start line for the snowshoe races at Chestnut Mountain Ski Resort. I had come with my husband, Donald, and our daughter, Cathy, to see my 11-year-old grandson at the winter Special Olympics. Bobby was scheduled to compete in the 50 meter race today.

Yesterday we had waited in bitter cold to watch the preliminary 100 meter snowshoe trial. After the starter's pistol fired, Bobby got off to a slow start. The other competitors hurried up a small hill to the finish line. Confused and disoriented by the noise of the crowd, Bobby placed his hands over his ears. Finally he started walking the course. With his video camera trained on Bobby, Donald stood at the side of the course and yelled encouragement. "Go, Bobby, go!" When Bobby heard Pa's familiar voice, he detoured and walked straight to his grandfather. Although he was given a second chance,

Bobby failed to finish the 100 meter trial and was disqualified. An hour later he finished the 50 meter snowshoe trial and guaranteed himself a spot in today's competition.

Although he had spoken several words by his first birthday, Bobby lost all speech a few months later and began to exhibit the rocking and hand flapping motions common to autistic children. I was devastated by the diagnosis of autism. All my hopes and dreams of a normal life for him were gone. He would never hit a home run. He wouldn't graduate from college or dance with me at his wedding. And he would never hold a child of his own. Still, I never lost hope that he would talk again one day.

A respite worker named Ed Halverson always greets Bobby with the words, "Hi, friend." Because of his love for Ed, Bobby worked hard and learned to say "hi" a year ago. He still can't manage the word "friend." With encouragement from all of us who love him, he keeps trying. As Bobby purses his lips and blows, I purse my lips and blow with him. Sometimes I can hear the "f" sound, and I smile and praise him. "Good talking, Bobby! Good saying 'friend'!"

Despite bitter cold on this first day of February, the athletes waited patiently and courteously for their chance to compete. Those who could speak laughed and talked and cheered for their teammates. For the thousandth time I wished that Bobby could talk. Then I remembered the special ways that Bobby expresses affection. All he needs to do is throw his arms around my neck and flash his beautiful smile and I'm a goner. Sometimes, as we sit on the couch watching TV, he rests his head on my shoulder and reaches for my hand. The warmth of his touch fills me with indescribable joy and peace.

Dear God, I couldn't possibly love him more than I do. I know that You love us with all of our imperfections. How could I not love and accept this sweet boy just the way he is? Thank you for sending Bobby to us.

At last it was time for Bobby to compete. This would be the final 50 meter race and the end of the day's competitions. With hope in my heart I watched him join four boys and wait for the race to begin. As Bobby's coach suggested, Cathy stood at the finish line where she could shout encouraging words to keep him going. When the starter's gun fired, four boys made a fast start over the snow and headed up the hill. Bobby stood alone at the start line. He looked from side to side as if he didn't know what to do. As two hundred voices cheered him on, he covered his ears with his hands. Finally he dropped his hands, looked straight ahead and plodded slowly up the middle of the course. Time stopped as he took one painstaking step at a time. Halfway up the hill he was alone on the course. There was a long way to go. He looked so small, so lost, but he kept going. *Please God, I prayed. Please help Bobby make it.*

Cathy waved and yelled, "Come on, Bobby. Come to Mama." The crowd continued cheering. When Bobby spotted his mom, he walked toward her with a big smile. As he crossed the finish line, Bobby looked in his mother's eyes and grabbed her hands. Tears of joy filled my eyes, my heart overflowing with love and pride for my daughter and the brave grandson who wouldn't give up.

Although Bobby was the last in his group to finish, he received a medal. There are no losers at Special Olympics. Where there is love, we're all winners.

ABOUT THE AUTHOR

Barbara Voegeli grew up in Greensboro, North Carolina.

At age 13 she won the city-wide spelling bee championship and runner up in the state finals. She graduated from Greensboro Senior High School as a member of "Torchlight", a coveted honor similar to the National Honor Society.

In 1959 she left Greensboro for training at nationally famous Weaver Airline Personnel School in Kansas City. Upon graduation, she was immediately selected by American Airlines and was assigned to their Chicago office.

A few years later she married and was blessed with three children. Her love for children began a wonderful period as a nursery school teacher in

Highland Park, Illinois. Still thirsty for formal education in child care, she attended the College of Lake County and graduated with an associate degree. She was awarded a National Honor Society certificate for her straight A's and was a member of Phi Theta Kappa.

Her scholastic achievements led to a scholarship at National College of Education in Evanston, Illinois. Again, a National Honor Society recognition and member of Kappa Delta Pi.

In 1979 Barbara graduated from National College with a Bachelor of Arts in Education and a K-9 teaching certificate. She wrote hundreds of poems, received awards from Highland Park Poetry, and had short stories published. Barbara researched her Jessup family origins stemming from Yorkshire, England in 1579 and ancestors to the current year including a Revolutionary War hero and a Civil War soldier.

She became quite a professional level seamstress, making hundreds of blankets for the Linus Foundation, prayer shawls with a local church group, many sweaters and clothes for her grandchildren and future great-grandchildren. She was an accomplished piano player and wrote her own music. She was blessed with a beautiful soprano voice and sang with multiple church choirs. She also took up painting and did some very good oil and watercolor paintings.

Barbara Jessup Voegeli passed away on May 24, 2020.

The song title ' Close to You', was placed on the cover in memory of Brian, who died in 1972 at two years of age.

This was Barbara and Brian's song.

This book is being published in her memory by her husband Donald and daughter, Catherine.

AWARDS

Bios of Poets in the Illinois State Poetry Society

Barbara Voegeli

Most of **Barbara Voegeli's** poetry has been written in rhyme for her grandchildren. She took care of them three days a week for eight years and composed snapshots of the things they said and did at various stages of development. They are now eighteen (twin boy and girl) and a sixteen-year-old grandson. Whenever she reads the things she has written about them as they were growing up, it's like hitting the replay button as the experiences and words burst forth in living color. She is a graduate of the Children's Institute of Literature, and several of her pieces, both fiction and nonfiction, have been published. The only poem she has had published was the winner of the haiku challenge in the Project Linus Chicago/Northern Illinois Chapter contest two years ago. She has written a number of haiku and tanka poems and draws inspiration from walks by the Lake Michigan shore and through the outdoor rooms of the Chicago Botanic Garden.

Barbara observed the landscape on Oct 15, 2004 on our trip to Minnesota and wrote this Haiku.

Submitted to Highland Park Poetry in 2016 and won an award for Haiku. They made a poster of it for display

This certificate is awarded to

BARBARA VOEGELI

In recognition of her poem, "Song of the Shore" the selection for May 2015

Jennifer Dotson, Founder & Program Coordinator   1/24/15

Poetry That Moves is a collaboration of Highland Park Poetry and PACE, putting poetry on North Shore suburban buses operating between Evanston, Highland Park & Waukegan, Illinois

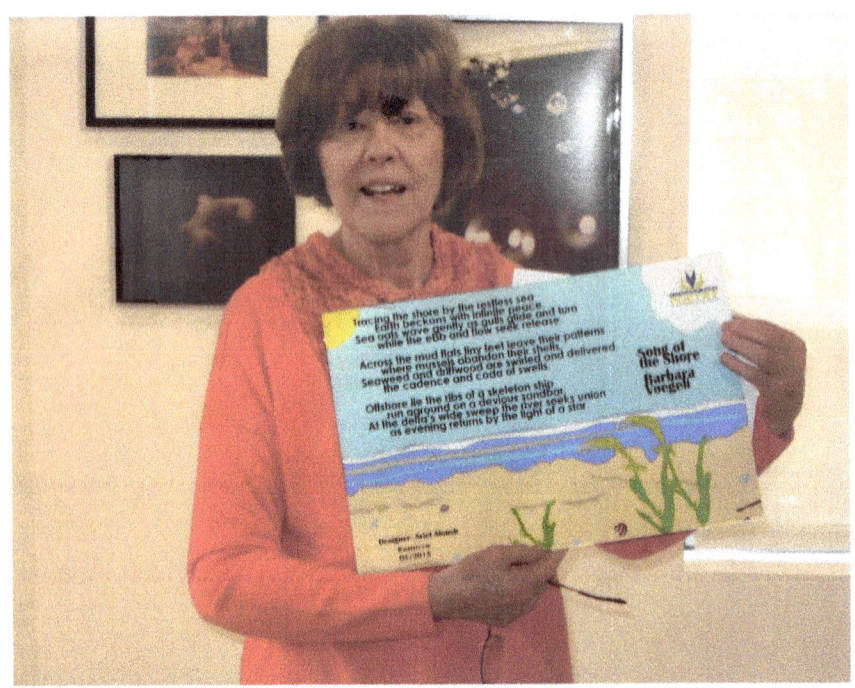

2016 Poetry Challenge
Shakespeare / Sonnet / Night

This certificate is awarded to

Barbara Voegeli

Her poem *haiku* "*black velvet curtain*" is Awarded

2nd Place

In the *Night* Category for Highland Park Resident Poet

Signature 4/1/16

Scarlet

Scarlet
Dramatic, fiery
Pulsating, radiating, exploding
Leaps from palette to creation
Crimson

1st prize winner Cinquains/Highland Park Resident – Poetry Challenge 2014
Honorable Mention in Colors category/Highland Park Resident

2014 Poetry Challenge
Colors / Fairy Tales & Legends / Cinquains

This certificate is awarded to

Barbara Voegeli

Her poem *Scarlet* is Awarded

1st Place in the Cinquains Category & Honorable Mention in the Colors Category for Highland Park Resident

Signature 4/18/14

www.ingramcontent.com/pod-product-compliance
Lightning Source LLC
Chambersburg PA
CBHW071853090426
42811CB00004B/595